GLIMPSE

GLIMPSE

SELECTED APHORISMS

GEORGE MURRAY

MISFIT

ECW Press

Published by ECW Press
2120 Queen Street East, Suite 200, Toronto, Ontario, Canada M4E 1E2
416.694.3348 / info@ecwpress.com

LIBRARY AND ARCHIVES CANADA CATALOGUING IN PUBLICATION

Murray, George, 1971-
Glimpse : selected aphorisms / George Murray.

ISBN 978-1-55022-981-3

I. Title.

PS8576.U6814G55 2010   C811'.6   C2010-901252-6

Editor for the press: Michael Holmes / a misFit book
Cover design: David Gee
Text design: Tania Craan
Printing: Coach House   1   2   3   4   5

The publication of *Glimpse: Selected Aphorisms* has been generously supported
by the Canada Council for the Arts, which last year invested $20.1 million in writing and
publishing throughout Canada, by the Ontario Arts Council, by the Government of
Ontario through the Ontario Book Publishing Tax Credit, by the OMDC Book Fund, an
initiative of the Ontario Media Development Corporation, and by the Government of
Canada through the Canada Book Fund.

 Canada Council for the Arts   Conseil des Arts du Canada   Canada   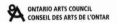 ONTARIO ARTS COUNCIL CONSEIL DES ARTS DE L'ONTAR

PRINTED AND BOUND IN CANADA

ECW PRESS
ecwpress.com

———

Everything has been said before, but since nobody listens
we have to keep going back and beginning all over again.
—André Gide, *Le Traité du Narcisse*

The splinter in your eye is the best magnifying-glass.
—Theodor W. Adorno, *Minima Moralia*

———

1

There is no way to forget any moment, except in its sequence.

2

As with the knife, the longer the conversation, the less frequently it comes to a point.

3

Do not discount the stupid bravery of the first to arrive.

4

The butterfly's wings are nothing to the overwhelming force of the common.

5

Knowledge is what happens when you rob suspicion of doubt.

6

One should always arrive before a tribunal naked, wearing only the first few words of the truth, or the last of a good lie.

7

Until you've seen some sign of your prey, you're not hunting, you're walking.

8

Mathematics is what happens to life when you shed the emergent complications of consciousness.

9

Those who have time to tell stories in the dying moments of our attention are also those who will be forgotten.

10

Rubble becomes ruin when the tourists arrive.

11

The one-legged bird is not so bad off.

12

Faith is a room with more exits than entrances.

13

Prayer, the soul's restless leg, is mostly harmless—except in how its relentless thumping below the mind's table distorts what's being written above.

14

Meaning is overflow from *trying*.

15

The definitions of *original* and *unique* change, depending on the number of people present.

To those who wonder whether the strangers we see in our dreams are actually other dreamers, I say, it is more urgent to wonder whether the strangers we see in our waking hours are actually other people.

Writing the erotic poem is like ironing in the nude—sexy for women, dangerous for men.

Panic is worry on a tight schedule.

To be mean requires a certain thoughtlessness; to be cruel, the opposite.

Anger without determination is just resignation.

21
___

Chaos occurs when habits overlap but refuse to form an ecosystem.

22
___

Culture is a physics of the self, in quantity.

23
___

Beauty is found with a quick glance; the grotesque is found by close study.

24
___

Somehow I can imagine being struck screaming much more easily than being struck dumb—but in the end, both are simply speechless, I suppose.

25
___

Anyone who yells loud enough can be famous among the pigeons.

Luck: being born with two lazy eyes that wander the same way.

DNA rhymes with *T and A*.

Children are only surprised by changes other than their own; for adults it's the exact opposite.

The first-born drives himself into the world like a nail without a head.

Dirt is what we heap upon enemies; loam our dead; earth our children.

31

Routine breeds sameness, shields mediocrity, and creates happiness.

32

Standards fall like pants: easily and on their own, once past a certain point.

33

Playing is what spectators do when they forget they're watching.

34

In the thriller, the worst thing that can happen to the hero is death. The more literary a novel gets, the further down the list of undesirable fates death falls.

35

The shortest distance between any two points is regret.

36

Angst is the larval form of boredom.

37

Are martyrs still martyrs when everyone's suffering?

38

The head of this pin has left holes in my feet.

39

Faith's only enemy is opportunity.

40

Is chance that which we *didn't* expect or that which we *couldn't* expect?

You are in your element when you don't know who will next walk through the door but you're confident that whoever it is will be just fine.

Art is an arranged marriage between chance and humanity.

Writing is the mention of myself to myself.

We're already being studied by the future.

If nostalgia had an address, it would be located at the intersection of Regret and Pity.

46

Terror is to falling what horror is to sinking.

47

The failed come-on is the successful brush-off.

48

The thicker the moustache, the more awkward the pickup line.

49

Only husbands and bad poker players bet on their whims.

50

The hotel is where potential and sadness conduct their affair to produce renewal.

51

The universe without life is a base state from which expectation arises.

52

Life is a manifestation of expectation; it is nature anticipating a question and coming up with an answer.

53

Failures are usually only noticeable when they happen in tandem rather than accumulating over time, like grass.

54

The prime struggle: finding out how to spend your time instead of having it spent for you.

55

The universe remains mum on the subject of itself, yet still we hold the mic to its lips as though waiting for comment.

56

Truth is whatever piece of information would have been useful to have before the conversation began.

57

Knowledge is as permanent as you; and sometimes as permanent as us.

58

Comparison is the way we create a world that would be free of the idea of itself without us.

59

When strangers acknowledge one another it is always in the brotherhood of condition.

60

The first level of charity is imagining the needy.

61

Children know as much about violence as their parents allow, plus whatever their parents have forgotten was included at birth.

62

It's not in my heart to commit murder, though it may very well be in my hands.

63

We try to understand ourselves by adding the subjective to the objective, a favour we don't grant to anything else in the physical universe. Yet, if we are part of, and created by, the physical universe, are we then either overestimating our uniqueness or missing something greater about everything else?

64

Love evolved from sex, but passed through grooming first.

65

Only the foolish carry candles into a night in which they plan to sleep.

66

The good news is: you're loved. The bad news is: so are your enemies.

67

It's not easy to be me, but I know that's true for you, too.

68

On the boat you lean over the rail looking in all directions to find a better view, but you'd really be easier to please below decks, looking out the porthole, offered an option of one.

69

All writing is a bit like wearing a toupée—those who can get away with it do, but those who can't look like fools. Poetry, in turn, is like jogging in a toupée . . .

70

These days, I can barely remember ourselves.

71

Manners are inherited answers to inherited problems.

72

You cannot say you know someone whose dreams you cannot imagine.

73

There's what we hope to do, what we dream of achieving, and what we actually do on days when the first two aren't happening.

74

Turning forty is like looking up and realizing it's two in the afternoon.

75

That which is best under certain conditions, and at a certain time, is also good only then as well.

76

The blatant inequity of beauty is bothersome—not so much that some are while others aren't, but rather that one is allowed near while another is left to the grotesque.

77

Allure is a blanket not appropriate for the weather; lust is a pillow only comfortable in one position; love is a mattress too soft at first and then, as the body adjusts, never again soft enough.

78

You can judge entire societies by the expressions on the faces of their dolls.

79

Beauty will always remain hidden, because one cannot look deeper than the skin—at least not without opening it.

80

The sad thing about "priceless" is it can also mean "worthless."

A culture is a coincidence of like-minded individuals. *Culture* occurs when these people find out they don't all agree.

Revellers feel insulted by one who doesn't join them, even if he wasn't invited.

Stupid can be really good if stupid is on your side.

Distraction is a form of absolution.

Only a beard can change your face more than religion.

I'm sometimes disappointed by plenty, but too satisfied to do anything about it.

When faced with difficulty, it's not interesting to wonder whether you could have saved yourself the trouble by choosing a different path in life, but rather how you'd have handled this situation if you'd arrived here by any other road.

The difference between curse and legacy is time.

Suspicion and evidence are always holding the elbows of intuition.

The only bad thing about luck is that we don't get to choose how it's applied.

91

Models have that vacant look because they aren't allowed to stare back.

92

The view is forever doing more than half its work behind us.

93

Even fully dressed, some people wear nothing but the fingerprints of others.

94

We live in a time when attention is subsidized by habit.

95

The universe, like fashion, will come around to a point like this again. Whether or not it should.

96

The problem with panic is that it lasts an infinite span in a short time.

97

For the drunk, every opening of an eyelid is onto a lover.

98

Harmony is coincidence harnessed.

99

Satiety is a leaky boat under constant repair.

100

The body is what happens when the mind wanders.

The secret club is a social tool to keep separate those who contribute best through their absence.

Solipsists should mind their own business.

She looks like a million bucks, but it's all in fives.

The slot machine is the idiot's ATM.

The poem doesn't mimic life because nothing about the poem is random.

106

Myth is just how consciousness handles instinct.

107

Nothing but doubt can hold my attention; nothing but attention can ease my doubt.

108

Each book is a paper mind that can no longer learn.

109

Compulsion is where habit meets need.

110

The lyric has all writing for context; melody has only the world.

III

Getting old doesn't bother me, but staying old does.

112

Wisdom is truth run through perspective, and boredom.

113

Heuristics rhymes with *fishsticks*.

114

Beauty is a matter of being too distracted to find flaws.

115

Just like the scar hidden beneath the hairline, so too do all predilections become apparent with age.

Death cannot be infinite, by virtue of life's interruption. Nothing with a starting point can be considered infinite.

They put crosswords in with the obituaries as a reminder.

The cat in the box, whether dead or alive, is definitely the universe being the universe.

Teach your child to find his own pulse, and you'll both suddenly realize how near his blood flows to the air.

To the wind, an open window is a drain.

What do you sacrifice when you look away from the horrific? The answer.

Measure stitches ineffable moments of common understanding to language.

Shadow, not light, is the language of the sun.

Effort is the mother of justice, but also the sister of disappointment, and the whore of waste.

Time occurs as rival *nows* bully each other.

126

Expectation is how things happen; chance how they come true.

127

Nows are the molecular form of fundamental *thens*.

128

To the true pessimist, everyone else is an optimist.

129

Death is a relinquishing of the prerogative to object.

130

Time is a tea through which your life's water is only run once.

Embarrassment is regret in its youth.

If there are psychics among us, they have great poker faces.

Dignity has no place in dying, but plenty of room in death.

I never get motion sickness until I stop moving.

Being is like a rising tide: there's only so long you can stand in the shallows before you're forced to retreat, float, or swim.

136

Any set of circumstances will attain consciousness once they become complex enough.

137

Sod is civilization's kudzu.

138

What makes your particular numbness preferable to all others?

139

I'm not the me you know, though I understand your suspicion—because I suspect it too.

140

Flux is a state in which *id* is replaced with value *x*.

141

In the infidelity of a wish, it's not the glance or the eyebrow that betrays, but the effort.

142

Indigestion occurs when you break your stomach's heart by cheating on her with your mouth.

143

The waitress looks like a million dollars, but you're a rich man already, and sure the problem with men is how little they know about anything but making more money.

144

Your intention is a single rail of train track stretching into the distance.

145

Watch where you spend your inheritance of attention; every purchase of the eyes is non-refundable.

146

My faith in the chance of success has changed to a suspicion that failure is a natural state, like bodies at rest, unaffected by other forces, all things considered.

147

A little piece of God is a little bit of the Devil.

148

Heaven has never tipped under the weight of inequity, but would topple at a touch of equality.

149

The prophet requires an audience of people; the articulate prophet requires an audience of prophets.

150

You can have it all so long as you don't reach beyond your arms.

151

Looking is grooming from a distance.

152

Orgies are self-help groups for narcissists.

153

Turns are not as sexy as curves, if only because they can't be taken as fast.

154

The kiss that is an act between two becomes an object when only one knows it's been given.

155

Gravity has other plans for those who think love attracts.

156

The brain is also gut.

157

Gourmet: one culture's vice coupled to another's sustenance.

158

The gods are celebrities between projects.

159

Second thoughts are Easter Sundays of the mind.

160

Master plans rhymes with *disaster plans*.

161

The soul is a herd and thought is a shepherd, but reality is a fence and chance a border collie.

162

Whether or not you think a dog is smiling depends on how well you know the dog.

163

Unremembered moments are life's junk DNA—we seem to be able to operate fine without them, but they're surely there for a reason.

164

The artist obsessed with eyes is young; the one obsessed with seeing a little older; the one obsessed with what having seen has done to his eyes is eldest.

165

That's the thing with evolution, it's turtles all the way down.

166

Nature does danger, humans do threat.

167

Time's daughter is sequence.

168

What I'm supposed to do is always being lost to obligation.

169

Worship doesn't lead to salvation, it's just the process through which we notice it.

170

Hell isn't about fear or pain, it's about the removal of acclimatization—the withdrawal of the ability to cope.

171

The main difference between a priest and a preacher is who comes to whom.

172

What prefixes can you drop to make yourself happier?

173

Static isn't the absence of signal, but the absence of a single focus.

174

For the privileged, choices pile up, but like the same word in the mouth of many different speakers.

175

Charity is what we give to make things go away.

176

What's unique to the moment is unique to the moment just passed.

177

The addict is someone who passes from self-interest to more basic forms of need.

178

One can sense intelligence in others the way the contents of a pantry might be guessed at from the scents in the kitchen.

179

Sacred is what happens to questions when we can no longer stand to seek an answer.

180

Compulsion cannot be quantified, but is always about quantity.

181

The dog repays the extra long walk by rolling in twice as much shit.

182

In front it is the tie; behind it is the leash; above it is the noose; below it is the shackle.

183

Doing something right is not necessarily reason enough to do it again.

184

Every crowd is a mass grave that death never visited.

185

"No interest" is a position of potential to those who do not hold it.

Liars blink, leaders pause.

Anger is the credit card debt of the personality.

The days gone by that cannot be changed point to days ahead that cannot be changed.

The flag does not identify the nation, it identifies the wind.

The hourglass has a healthy attitude towards time: the sand falling through a few grains at a time repeats itself, never landing in the same arrangement, but even on inspection appearing close enough.

191

Death happens when you fall one way and your body falls another.

192

Is the soul rider, saddle, or horse? It is grass.

193

What a tourist sees depends less on where they are than who they are.

194

Digging a hole is dry land's version of bailing water.

195

Sound is like water: it gets into things.

196

The fate of the lake is to be transparent, but never seen through.

197

The gambler, like the hunter, is one whose fortunes rest on the confluence of chance and attendance.

198

When there is enough, there's also the unnecessary—abundance is not what's needed: it's what's possible.

199

Erosion is a kind of tailoring.

200

As we age we study anatomy by witnessing it fail.

201

There's not a single thing that couldn't be, but pretty much everything is next to impossible.

202

Shame is an authorial intrusion into the narrative you create of yourself.

203

It's best to work off the cuff when you have something up your sleeve.

204

A culture is a system for distinguishing successes and failures; a community is a system for discounting successes and failures; a cabal is a system for devising successes and failures.

205

Ignorance is an emergent property rising from intellect.

Being of reduced circumstances is only bad if you lead an uninteresting life.

The best lives have common beginnings and endings, but different middles.

We gather in groups around languages as though each tongue were a campfire and silence were the cold.

Theory is what shepherds the pleasant surprise from idea to the grinding machinery of moment.

Heroes are the rogue waves of politics.

What causes ruin is that which survives ruin.

When one tries and is unable to adapt, we ridicule—yet when one refrains from change, we laud the bravery of the defiance.

All your mistakes can tell you is there's something to the idea things can be perfect.

The marriage of fools should be celebrated by all.

The line between envy and pity is a night's sleep.

216

There's nothing like the unexpected divorce of friends to remind you you're not watching closely enough.

217

Five years was twenty years ten years ago.

218

Clinging is climbing without ascent.

219

Does the desperate man see the health and happiness of others as less-than-possible or more-than-can-be-asked-for?

220

Every house bought from others is a ruin that must be reclaimed.

Drinking whiskey is a form of amputation; four fingers, three fingers, two fingers . . . Luckily, I have two hands.

The fast is a kind of charity to that which isn't eaten.

Acceptance is a matter of ignorance.

The reason I resist religion: I've never been confident enough to start my prayers with "Now I lay me down to sleep . . ."

I've warned you: if something goes wrong, I won't be held reliable.

226

The spending of money is a bucket brigade with no fire at the end.

227

The currency of a time without imagination is *solution*.

228

Every exit on the highway turns off to somewhere just fine.

229

Abundance is most appreciated when it's either new, or imaginable as an absence.

230

Taking the lead now means promptly getting in line.

231

Every shoulder is a gibbet from which the drunk hang.

232

If chance is in the landscape and Mankind in the highway, then God is in the traffic.

233

We do not fear the unknown, but rather that which we can imagine—that which we suspect might be, but cannot yet count on. The truly unknown is a cinch.

234

Define your worth by what you take from life when you leave it.

235

When we die we are finally impersonating no one.

236

The first sign of luxury is the doodle.

237

Relationships are like slot machines: the mere legend of jackpot payouts enough to keep people coming back.

238

Most times the only treasure we find on digging is the satisfaction of having picked a spot.

239

At every point on the mountain, you've conquered some other hill.

240

Some need no more stage than the curb.

241
─────

No number of glances can add up to a good look.

242
─────

The ideas of the moment are being squeezed out by the considerations of the day.

243
─────

The first choice is not the choice, but the choice to choose.

244
─────

Self-image is a mirror with no silver.

245
─────

Ask me what I want out of life and I'll tell you, more or less.

246

Being in one's element means, essentially, being alone.

247

Epiphany is a moment of revelation so intense it obliterates itself, like a storm that rips up the landscape, but also sweeps it clean.

248

Prayer can be any communication to which only one person is privy.

249

Conviction is worth the work of several pairs of scissors.

250

Discontent hangs in every mental closet like a little black dress.

251

One needn't be heard to be understood, only quoted.

252

Consciousness is the universe's attempt at knowing death.

253

Stepping stones both define the river's path and undercut its direction.

254

Every surface is a mirror if you force your shadow on it.

255

There is also a freedom to be had in the narrow window.

256

All silences are passive aggressive.

257

In actual chaos, anarchy represents order.

258

Gasp is where subsistence meets abstinence.

259

Mist is a rain that can't agree with itself.

260

God is the clawed hammer of the celestial tool kit; memory the photo fallen from the wall; reality the bent nail.

261

A fit of framing leads to a lifetime of misappreciation.

262

Is it that so much *new* has arrived or that what's finished is finally beginning to make its exit?

263

If his mind were wine he'd have spilled himself by now.

264

The time of your life requires a second hand.

265

My enemies will always remain obscure. To me.

266

On either side of awful stand revulsion and worship.

267

The cat that dies is simply the cat that lost count.

268

Every man is a dimension unto herself.

269

God can afford to be gentler and more understanding now that he's not responsible for everything.

270

On the highway of life each tongue is an on-ramp, each asshole an exit.

271

Immortality lasts only so long as life.

272

My rush is not born of impatience so much as suspicion.

273

Diversity is what happens when indecision and acceptance meet.

274

Memory is God's runaway child; its absence a sure sign the parent is near.

275

What the sad man has to say is about himself. What the dying man has to say is about the sad man.

The perfect friend is the silent enemy.

The night is so covered in full stops we cannot read the sentences for the periods.

If *living* is an art, *life* is a curated selection.

Children are the first to discover that making friends does not always mean making allies.

The idea of a meteoric rise is absurd.

281

The prey is free to move about at will, but the predator must always follow the prey.

282

The chances of something happening rest on whether you're looking for likelihood or livelihood.

283

Thoughts are bridges, not the traffic crossing them.

284

Bravery is not a thing of the moment, but something assigned on reflection.

285

When both fighters cross themselves before the bell how does God decide between?

There are perspectives I'll never have because the views from that point are blocked by those already doing the looking.

The misplaced journal or diary means thoughts lost; the misplaced pen means thoughts trapped.

Children are wedges of your apple, pared away one at a time until you disappear.

What the leaf protects from the sun is not the same as what it protects from the rain.

The universe is a table too wide to have corners.

291

Children are the bomb-sniffing dogs of the personality.

292

Anything that is spelled "t-w-o" but is pronounced "too" must be elegant.

293

You don't have to be good at colour commentary to talk a blue streak.

294

Every gift changes expectation; every theft as well.

295

Even if what you do is seminal, there is no guarantee it will be productive.

296

The gap in music is called a rest; in conversation a pause; in logic a flaw.

297

The penny found in the middle of the busy road presents an interesting test case.

298

Coincidence without you here is just incidence, lacking in both interest and potential.

299

What line will the edge not cross?

300

The unknown is most frightening when it becomes a possibility, but possibilities are least scary when they remain unknown.

301

If Noah came today, he'd be hard pressed to find two of each of us.

302

Worry is a playground for those with time enough to visit it.

303

Everyone works in sales now.

304

After happy hour, things get back to how they were—an overpriced sadness, or acceptance, which is just sadness without regret.

305

Triumph over death is only to be had in the moment of forgetting, when all other winnings come second to the victory of distraction.

306

Disgust and allergy are ailments of all but the truly poor.

307

The difference between a valley and shallow grave: one scenic, the other a scene.

308

The expectation of immortality for our unborn children is something we all have the opportunity to pass on.

309

The tears of the over-privileged are vestigial.

310

Subtract *have* from *need* to find *worth*.

311

Satisfaction starts to happen when you outrun your own tendency to run.

312

You can drown in a depth, but you'll never drown in meaning.

313

Justice is never black and white, except on cop cars and killer whales.

314

At the finish line, the mayor tells everyone they should be proud, but shakes the winner's hand alone.

315

The man who's lost all cannot look the one who has everything in the eye, but he who has never had anything has the longest stare, which no one can meet.

Nostalgia rises from the calming after life's argument, when you think of what you could have said, but cannot go back and fix; it's a small voice saying, "That right you're thinking of now is only another right's wrong," and you know you'd be where you are, regardless.

The line between stupidity and bravery is memoir.

Sleep is a lost and found of great thought.

Fantasy is everything others don't see in you.

Without the space between its elementary particles, a city of remarkable size fits into a matchbox—what a cataclysm of farsightedness then, our acceptance of the opaque.

321

The nerds will inherit the third rocky planet from the nearest M-class solar body.

322

Light is a universal solvent.

323

Evil happens like a woman who can talk while applying lipstick—seemingly effortlessly, but likely with a lot of practice.

324

Meaningless and *random* are seldom the same thing, even by chance.

325

Life is all about remembering yourself to death.

326

Any words not burnt are potential gospel.

327

The mercy of children is only as reliable as the cruelty of children.

328

I want to measure my seconds in miles, but I've only got a watch when what I need is a look.

329

Reading is like taking a poison and its antidote in the same swallow.

330

For the child, the lullaby's importance lies in its being sung; for the father it lies in how it may be sung without thinking.

All trains also head back in one direction.

Speaking is a privilege if we don't say it isn't.

The only reliable form of time travel is living.

Lies are not the opposite of truth; ideas are.

If a photo is a thousand words, what's the count on the look of the face in it?

336

Poetry is what translates the wordless scream of epiphany into the ability to forget.

337

I was born too late to know the work of naming the constellations, but not too late to have never seen them.

338

Sleep is the rough draft of death.

339

The only thing permanent enough to remain is the time after life, which comes and never ends, unlike that which came before, and during.

340

Jacob wrestled not to win, but to hold on.

341
———

Every day: unremembered anniversaries of eye contact.

342
———

Second to none does not mean the best, unless you believe in absences.

343
———

Like sides on a circle, there's only one end to the sea.

344
———

Any scarecrow is bound to be in a good position.

345
———

The tapped knee, like the mind, is a demonstration of reflex.

346

The Devil don't know half of what I know, and that's how I know I'm not half bad.

347

In a successful marriage it takes a lifetime of picking to scratch a seven-year itch.

348

Help is what happens to you when your need meets the need of another.

349

Those who have *aged* can look at old photographs and see themselves within. Those who have *aged well* can look in mirrors and see themselves within.

350

True happiness is inherited, but laterally.

We wipe mustard from our faces with hands, smiles with news.

Constructionism rhymes with *obstructionism*.

Novelists should be the opposite of kings, at least when it comes to *show* and *tell*.

Sunlight could not lie without the help of windows.

Did the hug evolve from the choke or the choke from the hug?

356

A line is both the shortest and the longest distance between two points.

357.

Complexities unnoticed remain simplicities.

358

A web is a spider's harp; every death its song.

359

An ideal situation: have and be no enemy. A practical ideal: have enemies but don't be the enemy of others.

360

Fishermen cast anchors before lines.

361

Happiness is something perceived from a vantage: a shallow valley or worn hill missed when travelled, but recognized from a proper perspective.

362

The smoothest pen leads to the messiest writing.

363

Love is like the screw fitting the nut: nothing unusual.

364

Just like the halved apple, the cut thought cannot roll away.

365

Those who cannot hear Nature's call end up pissed.

366

Falling asleep is not like falling down stairs; it's like falling up them.

367

If only we could apply collateral damage to the value of our estates.

368

I dream in a rhythm similar to that in which I court friendship: without a care for the most part, and of a sudden with intensity.

369

When I wonder what we'll do for dinner, I'm generally not worrying.

370

The trees on the edge of the forest are the ones with the most leaves.

If the purpose of the race is to win, then only one runner can truly finish.

The coffin's satin is life's pink slip.

Every pencil lead is a dryad.

In the city and the woods both, the scent of fire causes panic, but by the lake it only causes guitars.

The collective unconscious is a no-brainer.

Your friends are the people you forget to document your time with.

377

It takes a lot of ones to make up infinity, but oddly, infinity has no discernable ones in it.

378

There is some part of me that's eager to find out what I'll be like as an old man, perhaps a close cousin to that part of me that hopes I'll make it there.

379

Tragedy passes through sorrow and humour both on its way to comedy.

380

Both is the choice of kings.

381

The book acts as a whimsical translator for every reader's personal language.

382

True beauty is both massless and frictionless and will not only pass through all obstacles, but could not stop if it wanted to.

383

Stepping out from the well-lit lobby into full sunshine is a good, painful way to be reminded you don't know light.

384

How do you know which wall is the fourth?

385

The trouble with staging a comeback is the position you come back to.

386

It's painful to be a mistake in a time bored with error.

387

Marriage is an adjustable wrench—most people have one, but most also do very little with it.

388

The polar opposite of "poet" is "actor."

389

Nurses are those who separate the living from the still-living.

390

Depression is insanity without urgency.

391

If ambition is wishing on a star, reality is realizing one won't be enough.

392

Possible is the apartment futon on which Perhaps houses Maybe when he comes to visit.

393

You holiday with death for a while, then it's back to work.

394

It's only memory that requires time; recognition happens between moments.

395

Urgency is a product of pessimism.

396

Resolve to always be the last one clapping as the applause dies, and someday you'll also be the first as it begins.

397

Goethe was wrong: there *is* something worth more than this day. Tomorrow.

398

The darkness is always westward in the morning and you are always in somebody's east.

399

There is plenty we cannot say that can be thought; there is enough left unspoken to keep us thinking for years.

400

Forgetting what happened is also a part of what happened.

401

Nobody will ever know who I am, and that's okay, because in the end it's the same with everyone else.

402

In martyrs and poets both, the rumour of greatness is enough to stave off criticism.

403

It's not that there's nothing to regret, but that I've narrowed down what I can regret simply by having shown up.

404

There's no song left unsung, so long as someone who knows the tune remains conscious.

405

Seeking epiphany is like being locked in a game of cat and mouse where the cat is your head and your ass is the hole in the wall.

406

Fathers are answers to questions children may never ask.

407

Hindsight is 20/20, but only if you're looking back.

408

Facing your discontent and being unable to name it is the definition of failure.

409

Finished thoughts belong to the dead.

ACKNOWLEDGEMENTS

During the writing of this book, the author received
awards from the Canada Council for the Arts and the
Newfoundland and Labrador Arts Council for which he
would like to express gratitude.

Excerpts from *Glimpse* appear in *Hotel Amerika*, *Maisonneuve*
magazine, and *Peter O'Toole: A Magazine of One-Line Poems* and
on the *Harriet* blog from *Poetry* magazine.

The author wishes to thank James Richardson who
inspired and encouraged the publication of this work.